MIX
Papier aus verantwortungsvollen Quellen
Paper from responsible sources
FSC® C105338

Pravin Bhole

Digital Receipt System for Paperless Billing

Anchor Academic
Publishing

Bhole, Pravin: Digital Receipt System for Paperless Billing, Hamburg, Anchor Academic Publishing 2017

Buch-ISBN: 978-3-96067-146-6
PDF-eBook-ISBN: 978-3-96067-646-1
Druck/Herstellung: Anchor Academic Publishing, Hamburg, 2017

Bibliografische Information der Deutschen Nationalbibliothek:
Die Deutsche Nationalbibliothek verzeichnet diese Publikation in der Deutschen Nationalbibliografie; detaillierte bibliografische Daten sind im Internet über http://dnb.d-nb.de abrufbar.

Bibliographical Information of the German National Library:
The German National Library lists this publication in the German National Bibliography. Detailed bibliographic data can be found at: http://dnb.d-nb.de

All rights reserved. This publication may not be reproduced, stored in a retrieval system or transmitted, in any form or by any means, electronic, mechanical, photocopying, recording or otherwise, without the prior permission of the publishers.

Das Werk einschließlich aller seiner Teile ist urheberrechtlich geschützt. Jede Verwertung außerhalb der Grenzen des Urheberrechtsgesetzes ist ohne Zustimmung des Verlages unzulässig und strafbar. Dies gilt insbesondere für Vervielfältigungen, Übersetzungen, Mikroverfilmungen und die Einspeicherung und Bearbeitung in elektronischen Systemen.

Die Wiedergabe von Gebrauchsnamen, Handelsnamen, Warenbezeichnungen usw. in diesem Werk berechtigt auch ohne besondere Kennzeichnung nicht zu der Annahme, dass solche Namen im Sinne der Warenzeichen- und Markenschutz-Gesetzgebung als frei zu betrachten wären und daher von jedermann benutzt werden dürften.

Die Informationen in diesem Werk wurden mit Sorgfalt erarbeitet. Dennoch können Fehler nicht vollständig ausgeschlossen werden und die Diplomica Verlag GmbH, die Autoren oder Übersetzer übernehmen keine juristische Verantwortung oder irgendeine Haftung für evtl. verbliebene fehlerhafte Angaben und deren Folgen.

Alle Rechte vorbehalten

© Anchor Academic Publishing, Imprint der Diplomica Verlag GmbH
Hermannstal 119k, 22119 Hamburg
http://www.diplomica-verlag.de, Hamburg 2017
Printed in Germany

Abstract

Digital Receipt System is the paperless billing system which is conceptual prototype of a digital receipt system.In the designing of this project the basic idea is when making purching any type of material, equipment or accessories with the help of RFID card the trasaction information is automatically packaged and sent to a the administrator where it can be logged into the database.A database system allowed them to access their all trasaction information till the date.

In this system microcontroller is used which contains the RFID card numbers for the detection of RFID card there is RFID reader is used and to record the transaction information the microcontroller is interface with the store computer which is connected to the database system.

Contents

List of Figures   iii

List of Tables   iv

1 Introduction   **1**
    1.1 Top-Level Block Diagram 2

2 Basic Concept and Literature Survey   **3**
    2.1 California Stores Pilot NFC System Providing Electronic Receipts . . 5

3 Radio Frequency Identification and Detection   **9**
    3.1 Introduction to RFID 10
    3.2 How RFID works 10
    3.3 Types of RFID 10
    3.4 RFID Frequencies 11
    3.5 History and Key-Developments 11
    3.6 RFID Applications 13
    3.7 RFID reader Pin Layout 13
    3.8 RS 232 Interface Formate 14
    3.9 RFID Technical Parameters 14
    3.10 RFID v/s Barcodes 15
    3.11 Current Scenario and Future 16

4 8051 Microcontrollers   **17**
    4.1 8051 Family 18
    4.2 Comparison of 8051 Family Members 18
    4.3 Various 8051 microcontroller 18
    4.4 Features of 8051 20
    4.5 Memory Architecture 21
    4.6 History of 8051 and Key Development 22
    4.7 Applications 23
    4.8 Development Cycle 25
    4.9 Hex File Format 25

	4.10 Programmer/Burner	27

5 Interface Between RFID With 8051 Microcontroller(AT89c51) 30
    5.1   Interfacing Code 32

6 Database Management System and .Net Framework 37
    6.1   Database 38
    6.2   Terminology and Overview 38
    6.3   Applications and Roles 39
    6.4   Database Design and Modelling 40
    6.5   Database Models 41
    6.6   Database Storage 43
    6.7   Database Security 43
    6.8   .Net Framework 45
    6.9   Design Features 45
    6.10 Common Language Infrastructure(CLI) 48
    6.11 Security 49
    6.12 Availability 49

7 Main Circuit and Design 50

8 Testing Results 55

9 Conclusion and Future Scope 57

References 58

List of Figures

1.1	Top- Level Block Diagram	2
2.1	Digital Receipt on Mobile	6
3.1	Radio Frequency Identification and Detection Tag	9
3.2	RFID Tag	12
3.3	RFID reader Pin Layout	13
3.4	Interfacing Diagram of RFID reader	15
3.5	RFID v/s Barcodes	16
4.1	8051 Microcontrollers	17
4.2	Block Diagram of 8051 Microcontrollers	21
4.3	Pin Diagram of 8051 Microcontrollers	24
4.4	Development Cycle by IDE	26
4.5	Hex File Format	26
4.6	Interfacing Between PC and Microcontroller	28
5.1	Interface Between RFID With 8051 Microcontroller	31
6.1	Collage of Five types of Database	42
6.2	The .NET Framework Stack	46
6.3	Visual overview of the Common Language Infrastructure(CLI)	48
7.1	Circuit of Digital Receipt System	50
7.2	Model of Digital Receipt System	52
7.3	LOGIN	52
7.4	HOME	53
7.5	INVOICE	53
7.6	ADD USER	54

List of Tables

4.1	Comparison of 8051 Family Members	18
4.2	Various of 8051 From Atmel (All ROM Flash)	19
4.3	Various Speed of 8051 From Atmel	20
4.4	Various of 8051 From Dallas Semiconductor	20
5.1	Interfacing of RFID With Microcontroller	31
7.1	Component List	51
8.1	Power Supply Section	55
8.2	RFID Section	55
8.3	LCD Section	55

Chapter 1

Introduction

The implementation of Radio Frequency Identification (RFID) technology in industrial manufacturing and retail supply chain management has seen strong growth in recent years. This is partly due to Wal-Marts RFID mandate to its suppliers. As more companies along the global supply chain adopt RFID, RFID tags embedded can be expected to proliferate in virtually every industrial product, ranging from computers to automobiles, in the near future. Large retailers like Wal-Mart and government agencies such as the U.S. Department of Defense (DoD) have driven recent developments in RFID technology. This in turn has a diffusion effect on hundreds of suppliers and manufacturers as their products are required to be tagged before shipping to these giant customers.

RFID technology provides a good alternative to automatically reading and writing product information. In addition to recording the identity of an object, RFID technology also documents its current status, recent past, and immediate future. Using modern identification techniques, production systems can now produce variants of a product, or even different products, at a batch size of one. A product with an RFID tag can be viewed as an intelligent product. Several studies in this emerging field indicate the necessity of adopting new manufacturing approaches for making intelligent products .

Digital receipt system is a conceptual prototype of paperless receipt. The basic idea is when we making a purchase with cash, magnetic card or RFID card the trisection information is automatically packaged & sent to a data base & store in it.

This project can be implemented on any store like component store, medical store or at which we have to create & maintain the records of purchasing and sales of products.

1.1 Top-Level Block Diagram

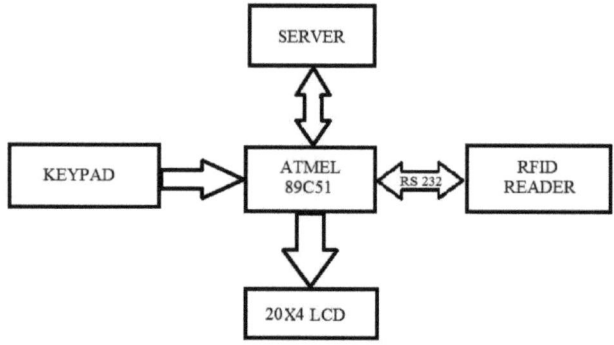

Figure 1.1: Top- Level Block Diagram

Our project contains hardware as well as software part of engineering in which MCU, card reader, LCD display and programming of project is belongs to hardware part & Data base controlling software is belongs to software part.

If someone wants to modify our project with high level usage then the project can also implement in the collage library & at the main entrance of the collage also. That is for the maintain the attendance records that how much time student or teachers present in the library or in the collage. All they need to do is at the in time they need to swipe his/her card to the stripe reader & the entry records of the date & time of the student or teacher will store at the date base.

Our project is also compatible with the barcode system or Q-code system if it can be modified or improve.

Chapter 2

Basic Concept and Literature Survey

E-commerce (electronic commerce) is the combination between the traditional business & the improvement of information processing brought by the internet. This combination allows companies to exchange sales information, do financial transactions, deliver goods & services and process invoices in an automatic way. E-commerce is leveraged by a safe communication medium which potential world-wide buyers can easily access.

Some of the biggest advantages of e-commerce (B2C and B2B) to a company are:

- Brings world-wide visibility: the business is available anytime, anywhere.

- Reduces the values associated with the consumer/ supplier or partner/partner transactions.

- Reduces product delivery time.

- Allows access to new markets with small financial effort.

- Reduces competitive advantages of big companies over the small ones: a portal does not depend on the companys financial strength; the client buys from the most trustworthy supplier and from the one who serves the client better.

- Reduces the bureaucracy associated with a purchase.

- Obtains information directly from a CRM (Customer Relationship Management): e.g. the customers personal tastes and the market evolution.

- Keeps the company permanently in touch with its business partners, thus increasing both ends satisfaction and diminishing communication costs.

A particular kind of traditional business where e-commerce may be beneficial is store commerce. Typically store commerce involves human interaction, waiting in line, the transaction of money and dealing with paper receipts and invoices. With these factors economic, time and ecologic issues emerge. E-commerce is a simple solution for these problems that can potentially bring a huge profit margin.

Studying how intelligent environments can help customers make the best purchasing decisions has become an important research area. One research issue in particular is to try and understand how mobile devices can help users to shop intelligently and intuitively.

An important aspect of shopping is the receipt that is given to customers. The customer may find the paper receipt less than ideal for a number of reasons: it can be easily lost, damaged or destroyed. This could be a problem when the customer wishes to use the paper receipt to organize his personal finances or to exchange the item of purchase. If the receipt is damaged to a point where its longer valid, the customer may not be able to properly document or manage his accounting. Therefore, an improved system that keeps digital receipts of commercial transactions would be beneficial.

The main goal of this project is to develop and implement a system of digital receipts for local transactions in commercial spaces, thus suppressing the need for paper receipts and reducing costs for business entities. This system will likely include the establishment of a connection between the mobile device of the customer and the fixed terminal in the store, and the transmission and storage of the receipt.

We are considering different ways of implementing this system. For example, we could use a smart-card (a pocket-sized card with embedded integrated circuits) or a device with a display such as the Open Moko phone or the G-phone.

The development of this project assumes that the creation of the digital receipt is independent of the means of payment and that the required data will be available to fill the receipt properly. In the final phase of the work, it should be possible to study the impact and acceptance of such a system by the merchants, institutions and customers.

2.1 California Stores Pilot NFC System Providing Electronic Receipts

By Claire Swedberg

Jan. 31, 2012-California startup Proximiant reports that a dozen San Francisco Bay Area stores arepiloting its Near Field Communication (NFC)-based system at the point of sale (POS), enabling shoppers to receive receipts, coupons, loyalty points and store credits on their mobile phones. By late spring 2012, approximately 1,000 stores are expected to participate, according to Fang Cheng, the company's cofounder and CEO. Since the pilots began in December 2011, stores' customers have been able to use an NFC-enabled phoneor an NFC-based Proximiant RFID card paired with a non-NFC phoneto download purchase receipts or discount coupons. After installing the Proximiant application on the phone, a customer can tap the NFC phone or card against a transceiver at the point of sale, thereby eliminating the need for paper receipts, coupons or loyalty cards.

Cheng says she conceived the idea in 2010, while traveling for business. She typically traveled between the Bay Area and New York every two weeks, and managed an expense account to pay for the various costs incurred during the trips. However, she says, collecting and storing all of the receipts became so cumbersome that she had a tendency to simply pay for the expenses herself, rather than be bothered with keeping receipts. She began to investigate whether NFC could provide a solution.

Not only could an electronic receipt system based on NFC technology save time and trouble for consumers, she explains, but it could also make it easier for merchants to offer customers discounts or loyalty programs. In addition, Cheng notes, there was also the green aspect of using an electronic solution to consider: If she could offer a service for delivering receipts electronically, she could eliminate the need for all of the paper collected and then discarded by shoppers.

Figure 2.1: Digital Receipt on Mobile

Cheng launched the company in March of last year with two other cofounders, and the trio then focused on developing a solution. The partners outsourced the design of the NFC POS device and NFC cards to a third-party contractor, and built the software to manage the read data, as well as a phone app for storing and displaying receipts, coupons and loyalty points.

To utilize the system, a merchant can visit Proximiant's Web site and request the service, which is currently free for those businesses piloting the technology. Beginning next month, the cost will be $50 for the device with a built-in RFID reader (developed for Proximiant) and 500 consumer NFC cards (made with NXP Semiconductors' 13.56 MHz passive RFID NFC chips) in the form factor of a key fob. There will also be a $14.99 monthly fee to manage read data, including the storage of each transaction, with a lower fee for every additional device used. The reading device can be plugged directly into the POS terminal, similarly to a receipt printer, and the store can then download Proximiant's driver software.

Most consumers do not yet have NFC-enabled phones, Cheng notes. Therefore, stores can provide customers with a Proximiant key fob with a built-in passive NFC RFID inlay, at no cost. Users who have a cell phone can then download the Proximiant app to their phone for free, by visiting the iTunes or Android Market app store. After installing the app, the user inputs the six-digit serial number on the back of the key fob, which then pairs the phone to the fob in Proximiant's server. A participant need not provide any personal information, since the data is simply linked to the phone rather than to a specific individual using it. When a purchase is made at any participating store, once the transaction is complete, the screen on the POS device lists the items purchased, along with their cost and the total amount due, and invites the customer to tap his or her phone or card against the device in order to receive a receipt. The patron can tap the key fob or NFC-enabled phone within 5 centimeters (2 inches) of the readerthe fob's RFID inlay can be read through a wallet, so the fob can be kept in a wallet if the consumer so choosesand the transaction data will then be stored on the phone.

For those with NFC-enabled mobile phones, the data is now stored on their phones, and they can simply scroll through the records to view their receipts. For those using the fob, the information is sent to the phone via an SMS connection. In either case, the phone must be powered on to receive receipts.

The consumer can utilize the Proximiant phone app to later retrieve a receipt by entering the store's name or the date, or simply scroll through the receipts listed. To return an item for exchange or refund, the shopper can present the receipt on the phone to the merchant, who can employ a bar-code scanner to read the bar code displayed on the electronic receipt. In the event that the store offers incentives, such as a discount for future purchases at that location, this data is also forwarded to the phone at the time of a transaction, and a user can redeem the discount at the point of sale, by presenting his or her phone to the merchant. The system also works for those who lack a mobile phone, Cheng says. For example, a consumer can still receive the NFC key fob, visit Proximiant's Web site and input the card's six-digit serial number to view an online record of receipts.

To date, Cheng says, most of the 12 stores have begun using the system only during the past few weeks, having opted to wait until after the Christmas sales season. However, she adds, the first store that piloted the solution reported that 90 percent of customers told about the technology chose to utilize it.

Consumers can not use the Proximiant app or card to pay for a purchaserather, they would pay for goods as they normally would have done without the Proximiant technology, using cash or a credit or debit card. The solution's value, Cheng says, is the elimination of receipts, the creation of a record of purchases (including each item within a single transaction) for finance management by the customer, and a channel through which merchants can extend loyalty programs and discounts. According to Cheng, the key fob can be used at the facilities of any participating erchant, enabling shoppers to employ the same system and app at multiple stores.

The stores piloting the Proximiant solution primarily represent fashion merchants, in addition to restaurants and other types of stores, such as bicycle-repair shops (where a record of tune-ups, for example, could be stored). Cheng says Proximiant is currently in discussions with universities across the United States regarding adopting the system for student use at college stores.

Chapter 3

Radio Frequency Identification and Detection

RFID is a tracking technology used to identify and authenticate tags that are applied to any product, individual or animal. Radio frequency Identification and Detection is a general term used for technologies that make use of radio waves in order to identify objects and people.

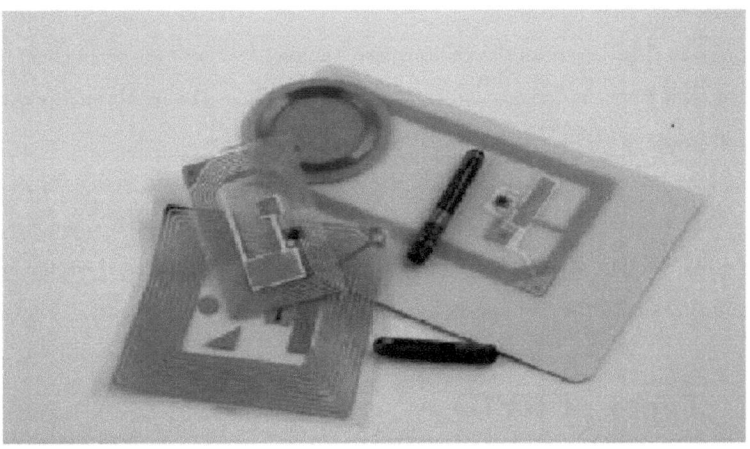

Figure 3.1: Radio Frequency Identification and Detection Tag

3.1 Introduction to RFID

Purpose of Radio frequency Identification and Detection system is to facilitate data transmission through the portable device known as tag that is read with the help of RFID reader; and process it as per the needs of an application. Information transmitted with the help of tag offers location or identification along with other specifics of product tagged purchase date, color, and price. Typical RFID tag includes microchip with radio antenna, mounted on substrate.

The RFID tags are configured to respond and receive signals from an RFID transceiver. This allows tags to be read from a distance, unlike other forms of authentication technology. The RFID system has gained wide acceptance in businesses, and is gradually replacing the barcode system.

3.2 How RFID works

Basic RFID consists of an antenna, transceiver and transponder. To understand the working of a typical RFID system, check the following animation.

Antenna emits the radio signals to activate tag and to read as well as write information to it. Reader emits the radio waves, ranging from one to 100 inches, on the basis of used radio frequency and power output. While passing through electronic magnetic zone, RFID tag detects activation signals of readers.

Powered by its internal battery or by the reader signals, the tag sends radio waves back to the reader. Reader receives these waves and identifies the frequency to generate a unique ID. Reader then decodes data encoded in integrated circuit of tags and transmits it to the computers for use.

3.3 Types of RFID

Active and passive RFID are different technologies but are usually evaluated together. Even though both of them use the radio frequency for communication between tag and reader, means of providing power to tags is different. Active RFID makes use of battery within tag for providing continuous power to tag and radio frequency power circuitry. Passive RFID on the other hand, relies on energy of radio frequency transferred from reader to tag for powering it.

Passive RFID needs strong signals from reader but signal strength bounced from tag is at low levels. Active RFID receives low level signals by tag but it can create higher level signals to readers. This type of RFID is constantly powered, whether in or out of the readers field. Active tags consist of external sensors for checking humidity, temperature, motion as well as other conditions.

3.4 RFID Frequencies

Just like you can tune a radio in various frequencies for listening to different channels, RFID readers and tags need to be tuned in to a same frequency for communication. RFID system uses various frequencies but most common and popularly used frequency is low, high and ultra high frequency. Low frequency is around 125 KHz, high is around 13.56 MHz and ultra high varies between 860-960 MHz Some applications also make use of microwave frequency of 2.45 GHz. It is imperative to choose right frequency for an application as radio waves work different at various frequencies.

3.5 History and Key-Developments

RFID has been around since II World War but was viewed as too limited and expensive in functionality for most of commercial use. With advancement in technology, cost of system components has reduced and capabilities have increased, making RFID more popular.

Lon Theremin invented a surveillance tool for Soviet Union in the year 1945. This tool retransmitted the incident radio waves along with audio information. Sound waves vibrated diaphragm that altered the shape of resonator, modulating reflected sound frequencies. This tool was not identification tag but a secret listening device.

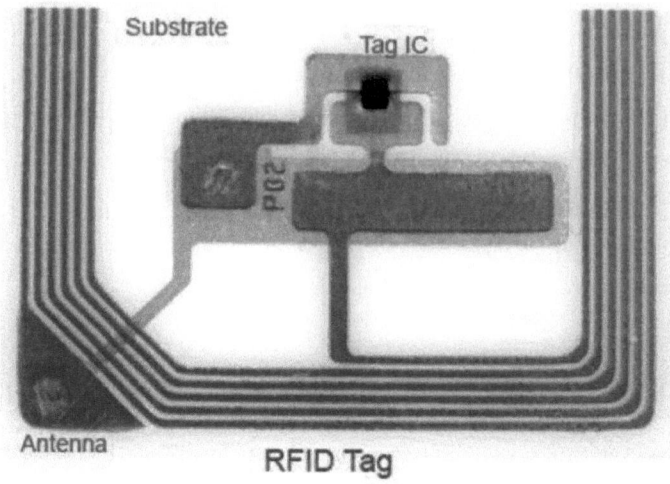

Figure 3.2: RFID Tag

But it is still considered as predecessor of the RFID technology due to it being energized, passive and stimulated by outside electromagnetic waves. Similar technology as IFF transponder was invented in UK in the year 1915 and was regularly used by allies in the II World War for identifying aircrafts as foes or friends. The transponders are used for by powered aircrafts till date.

Invented in 1973, device by Mario Cardullo is known to be a true ancestor of the modern RFID. Initially the device was passive and was powered by interrogating signals and had transponder 16 bit memory for application as toll device. The basic patent by Cardullo covers application of RF, light and sounds as the transmission media.

Early exhibition of the reflected power RFID tags, semi passive and passive was presented by Robert Freyman, Steven Depp and Alfred Koelle. This portable system used around 12 bit tags and worked at 915 MHz. And the first patent associated with abbreviation of RFID was approved to Mr. Charles Walton in the year 1983.

3.6 RFID Applications

The role of RFID is not just confined to Aircraft identification anymore; it is also lending a hand in various commercial uses. Asset tracking is one of the most popular uses of RFID. Companies are using RFID tags on the products that might get stolen or misplaced. Almost each type of Radio frequency Identification and Detection system can be used for the purpose of asset management.

Manufacturing plants have also been using RFID from a long time now. These systems are used for tracking parts and working in process for reduction of defects, managing production of various versions and increasing output. The technology has also been useful in the closed looped supply chains for years. More and more companies are turning to this technology for tracking shipments among the supply chain allies. Not just manufacturers but retailers also are using this RFID technology for proper placement of their products and improvements in the supply chain.

RFID also plays an important role in the access and security control. The newly introduced 13.56 MHz RFID systems provide long range readings to the users. The best part is that RFID is convenient to handle and requires low maintenance at the same time.

3.7 RFID reader Pin Layout

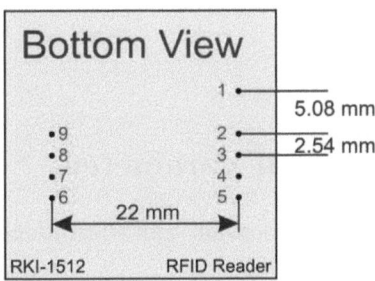

Figure 3.3: RFID reader Pin Layout

1. VCC 5V

2. GND

3. BEEP and LED

4. NC NOT CONNECTED

5. NC NOT CONNECTED

6. SET HIGH IS UART, LOW IS WEIGAND

7. TX UART TX

8. D1 WEIGAND DATA 1(OPTIONAL)

9. D0 WEIGAND DATA 0(OPTIONAL)

3.8 RS 232 Interface Formate

- 10 ASCII DATA card no.+ 2 ASCII DATA XOR result)

- Data baud rate:9600 bps

- Data bit8 bits

- Parity check: None

- Stop bit1

3.9 RFID Technical Parameters

The RFID reader is a standalone module with RFID reader and antenna. Its very small (32mmx32mm) in size and easy to integrate with any hardware design. It supports 125 KHz RFID tags and has DIP 0.1 pins to. Onboard antenna and hard plastic cover makes device small and sturdy. The module works on UART protocol

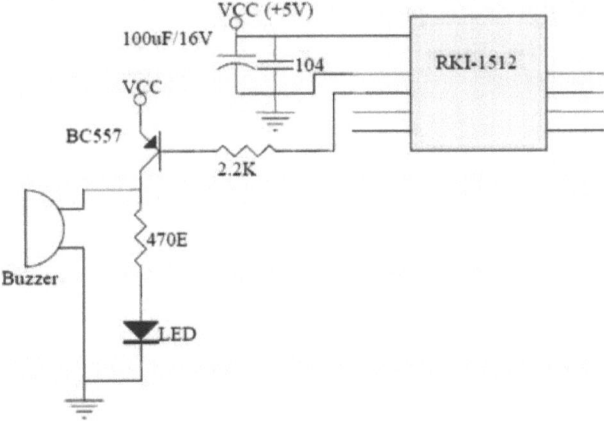

Figure 3.4: Interfacing Diagram of RFID reader

which allows user to integrate it with any PC or Microcontroller based design. It also supports Weygand protocol.

- Voltage : DC 5V

- Current : ¡50ma

- Operating Frequency : 125KHz

- Reading Distance : 5 CM, 10 CM (Maximum, only for special tags)

- Dimensions 32mm 32mm 8mm

3.10 RFID v/s Barcodes

RFID definitely has an edge over conventional technology of bar codes. RFID reader easily pulls data from tag at greater distances as compared to barcodes. Range in case of RFID is around 300 feet as against 15 feet of barcodes. So RFID tags can be read much faster as compared to barcodes. While reading the barcodes is time

Figure 3.5: RFID v/s Barcodes

consuming, RFID readers can interrogate rates of more than 40 tags in a second. Need of line of sight in case of barcodes restricts reusability and ruggedness of the barcodes. RFID, on the other hand are rugged, since its components are protected in plastic cover. The Radio frequency Identification and Detection can also be fitted within the products for ensuring greater reusability and ruggedness. Unlike barcodes, RFID tags can be used as write and read devices. One can use RFID tags for communicating with the tag and for altering the information stored on it.

3.11 Current Scenario and Future

Present trends point towards the fast growth of RFID in the next decade. With around 600 million RFID tags sold in the year 2005 alone, value of market including systems, services and hardware is likely to grow by factor of 10 between years 2006 -2016. It is expected that total number of RFID tags delivered in the year 2016 will be around 450 times as compared to the ones delivered in the year 2006.

Commercial applications using Radio Frequency Identification and Detection like logistics, transport, supply chain supervision, processing, manufacturing, medicine, access control are also likely to grow by leaps and bounds. But this smart technology will influence consumer sectors and government too. Barcodes and RFID will coexist for years to come, although the latter is expected to replace the former in many sectors.

Chapter 4

8051 Microcontrollers

A microcontroller is an economical computer-on-a-chip built for dealing with specific tasks, such as displaying or receiving information through LEDs or remote controlled devices. The most commonly used set of microcontrollers belong to 8051 Family. 8051 Microcontrollers continue to remain a preferred choice for a vast community of hobbyists and professionals. Through 8051, the world became witness to the most revolutionary set of microcontrollers.

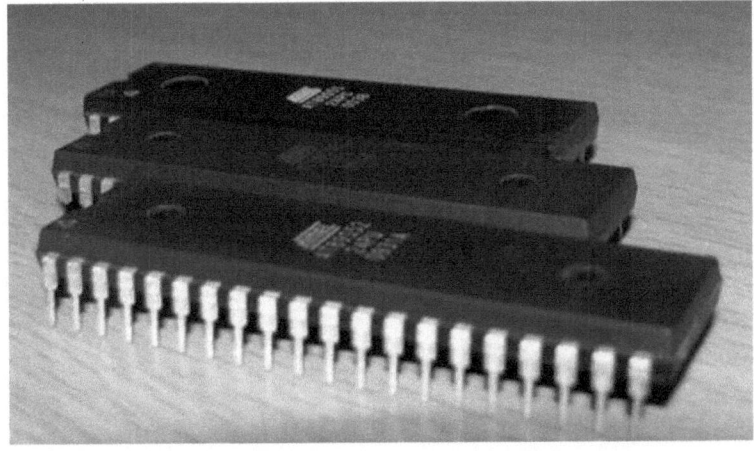

Figure 4.1: 8051 Microcontrollers

4.1 8051 Family

Intel fabricated the original 8051 which is known as MCS-51. The other two members of the 8051 family are:

1. 8052 This microcontroller has 256 bytes of RAM and 3 timers. In addition to the standard features of 8051, this microcontroller has an added 128 bytes of RAM and timer. It has 8K bytes of on chip program ROM. The programs written for projects using 8051 microcontroller can be used to run on the projects using 8052 microcontroller as 8051 is a subset of 8052.

2. 8031 This microcontroller has all the features of 8051 except for it to be ROM-less. An external ROM that can be as large as 64 K bytes should be programmed and added to this chip for execution. The disadvantage of adding external ROM is that 2 ports (out of the 4 ports) are used. Hence, only 2 ports are left for I/O operations which can also be added externally if required for execution.

4.2 Comparison of 8051 Family Members

Table 4.1: Comparison of 8051 Family Members

FEATURES	8051	8052	8031
RAM(Bytes)	128	256	128
ROM	4K	4K	8K
Timers	2	3	2
Serial Port	1	1	1
I/O Pins	32	32	32
Interrupt sources	6	8	6

4.3 Various 8051 microcontroller

8051 microcontrollers use two different kinds of memory such as UV- EPROM, Flash and NV-RAM. Hence 8051 will not be seen in the part number even though it is the most popular member of the 8051 family.

1. 8751:- This microcontroller is the UV-EPROM version of 8051. This chip has only 4K bytes of UV-EPROM. It is required to have access to the PROM burner and the UV-EPROM eraser to erase the contents inside the chip before it is programmed again. The disadvantage of using this memory is the waiting time of around 20 minutes to erase the contents in order to program it again. Due to this limitation, manufacturers fabricated flash and NV-RAM versions of 8051.

2. AT89C51 from Atmel Corporation:- Atmel fabricated the flash ROM version of 8051 which is popularly known as AT89C51 (C in the part number indicates CMOS). The flash memory can erase the contents within seconds which is best for fast growth. Therefore, 8751 is replaced by AT89C51 to eradicate the waiting time required to erase the contents and hence expedite the development time. To build up a microcontroller based system using AT89C51, it is essential to have ROM burner that supports flash memory. Note that in Flash memory, entire contents must be erased to program it again. The contents are erased by the ROM burner. Atmel is working on a newer version of AT89C51 that can be programmed using the serial COM port of IBM PC in order to get rid of the ROM burner.

Table 4.2: Various of 8051 From Atmel (All ROM Flash)

Part Number	ROM	RAM	I/O pins	Timer	Int	Vcc	Pack
AT89C51	4K	128	32	2	6	5V	40
AT89C52	8K	256	32	3	8	5V	40
AT89C1051	1K	64	15	1	3	3V	20
AT89C2051	2K	128	32	3	8	3V	20
AT89LV51	4K	128	32	2	6	3V	40
AT89LV52	8K	128	32	3	8	3V	40

3. DS5000 from Dallas Semiconductor: - Dallas Semiconductor fabricated the NV-RAM version of the 8051 which is known as DS5000. The PC serial port is utilized to load the program onto the in-built ROM.

Table 4.3: Various Speed of 8051 From Atmel

Part Number	Speed	Pins	Packaging	Use
AT89C51-12PC	12MHz	40	DIP Plastic	Commercial
AT89C51-16PC	16MHz	40	DIP Plastic	Commercial
AT89C51-20PC	20MHz	40	DIP Plastic	Commercial

There are different versions of packaging and various speed of the products mentioned in the above table.

Table 4.4: Various of 8051 From Dallas Semiconductor

Part Number	RAM	ROM	Timers	I/O pins	Int	Vcc	Pack
DS5000-8	128	8K	2	32	6	5V	40
DS5000-32	128	32K	2	32	6	5V	40
DS5000T-8	128	8K	2	32	6	5V	40
DS5000T-8	128	32K	2	32	6	5V	40

4. One - Time - Programmable (OTP) versions of the 8051:- This version of microcontroller is cheaper and available from various manufacturers. The manufacturers use OTP microcontroller for mass production because the price per unit is very cheap.

4.4 Features of 8051

The main features of 8051 microcontroller are

1. RAM 128 Bytes (Data memory)

2. ROM 4Kbytes (ROM signify the on chip program space)

3. Serial Port Using UART makes it simpler to interface for serial communication.

4. Two 16 bit Timer/ Counter

5. Input/output Pins 4 Ports of 8 bits each on a single chip.

6. 6 Interrupt Sources.

7. 8 bit ALU (Arithmetic Logic Unit)

8. Harvard Memory Architecture It has 16 bit Address bus (each of RAM and ROM) and 8 bit Data Bus.

9. 8051 can execute 1 million one-cycle instructions per second with a clock frequency of 12MHz.

This microcontroller is also called as System on a chip because it has all the features on a single chip The Block Diagram of 8051 Microcontroller is as shown in below Figure.

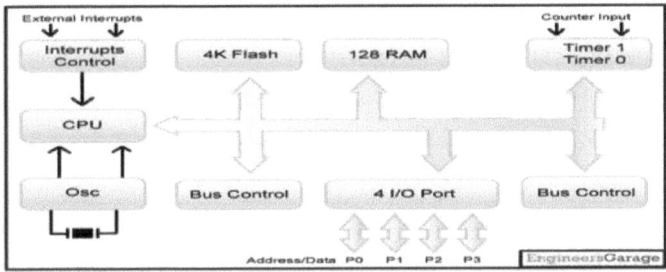

Figure 4.2: Block Diagram of 8051 Microcontrollers

4.5 Memory Architecture

The 4 discrete types of memory in 8051 are:

1. Internal RAM: - This memory is located from address 0 to 0xff. The memory locations from 0x00 to 0x7F are accessed directly. The bytes from 0x20 to 0x2F are bit-addressable. Loading R0 and R1 the memory location from 0x80 to 0xFF can easily accessed.

2. Special Function Registers (SFR):- Located from address 0x80 to 0xFF of the memory location. The same instructions used for lower half of Internal RAM can be used to access SFRs. The SFRs are bit addressable too.

3. Program Memory: - This is read only memory which is located at address 0. With the help of 16 bit Special Function Register DPTR, this memory can also save the tables of constants.

4. External Data Memory: - Located at address 0. The Instruction MOVX (Move External) should be used to access the external data memory

4.6 History of 8051 and Key Development

Intel Corporation fabricated the 8 bit microcontroller which was referred as MCS-51 in 1981. This microcontroller was also referred as system on a chip because it has 128 bytes of RAM, 4Kbytes of ROM, 2 Timers, 1 Serial port, and four ports on a single chip. The CPU can work for only 8bits of data at a time because 8051 is an 8-bit processor. In case the data is larger than 8 bits then it has to be broken into parts so that the CPU can process conveniently. Most manufacturers have put 4Kbytes of ROM even though the quantity of ROM can be exceeded up to 64 K bytes.

Intel permitted other manufacturers to fabricate different versions of 8051 but with the limitation that code compatibility should be maintained. This has added advantage that if the program is written then it can be used for any version of 8051 despite of manufacturer.

As years passed by, the quality of technology surpassed the expectation of the greatest minds, with gadgets becoming smaller, sleeker and more efficient. Microcontrollers were seen as the answer to the requirements raised in advanced electronics. This is the reason why manufacturers have now focused their production around the following main developmental aspects:

1. Ease-of-use

2. Market availability

3. Less power usage

4. Smaller processing power

5. More integrated features like RF and USB

6. Smaller form factors

4.7 Applications

The 8051 has been in use in a wide number of devices, mainly because it is easy to integrate into a project or build a device around. The following are the main areas of focus:

1. Energy Management: - Efficient metering systems help in controlling energy usage in homes and industrial applications. These metering systems are made capable by incorporating microcontrollers.

2. Touch screens: - A high number of microcontroller providers incorporate touch-sensing capabilities in their designs. Portable electronics such as cell phones, media players and gaming devices are examples of microcontroller-based touch screens.

3. Automobiles: - The 8051 finds wide acceptance in providing automobile solutions. They are widely used in hybrid vehicles to manage engine variants. Additionally, functions such as cruise control and anti-brake system have been made more efficient with the use of microcontrollers.

4. Medical Devices: - Portable medical devices such as blood pressure and glucose monitors use microcontrollers will to display data, thus providing higher reliability in providing medical results.

Formerly, programmers used machine language for coding. A machine language is a program that consists of 0s and 1s which was very dreary for the humans to program any computer. In due course of time, assembly language was developed in order to speed up the programming and make it error-free. Assembly language is a low level language which uses an assembler to translate the program into machine code. The high level programming languages such as BASIC, Pascal, Forth, C, C++, and Java are available to code the program for 8051. These high level languages make use of a Compiler to translate into machine code. For example, when a program is written in C, the program needs to be translated into machine language using C compiler. Usually, Assembly and C language is widely used for 8051 programs as compared to the other high level languages.

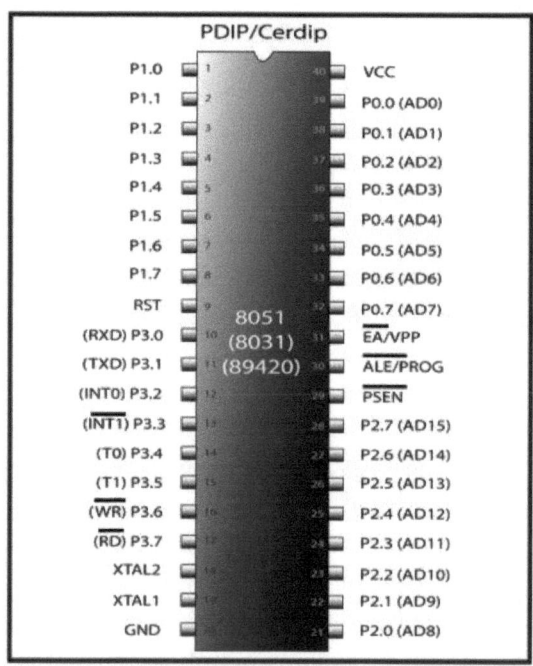

Figure 4.3: Pin Diagram of 8051 Microcontrollers

The 8051 provides a total of four ports for I/O operations. 8051 has 40 pins, of which 32 pins are set aside for the four ports. PO, P1, P2, and P3 each have 8 pins and can be used for either input or output. The remaining pins are designated as Vrt, GND, XTAL1, XTAL2, RST, EA, ALE/PROG and PSEN. 8051 allows you to manipulate one or all of the bits of a port, thus providing programmers with a unique and powerful feature. 8051 provides the programmer with the ability to read, write and modify each port to customize applications as much as possible.

4.8 Development Cycle

For developing or testing an embedded system application, a particular development cycle is followed which consists of several stages. An Integrated Development Environment (IDE) allows for implementation of all such steps of a development cycle. Typically, a development cycle has following steps:

1. The code is written/edited in an Editor program.

2. The Compiler/Assembler/Linker programs generate relevant support files like .hex, obj etc.

3. The code is loaded into Simulator/Debugger program.

4. The code is analyzed by Simulation or Debugging.

If an error occurs, the code is re-edited and the whole cycle is repeated.

4.9 Hex File Format

The Intel hex (ihex) generally known as hex file, is a format used to store machine language code in hexadecimal form. It is widely used format to store programs to be transferred to microcontrollers, ROM and EEPROM. The compilers convert the programs written in assembly, C etc into corresponding hex files, which are dumped into the controllers using burners/programmers. This article explores the details of

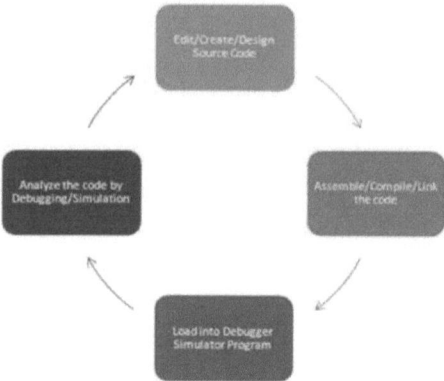

Figure 4.4: Development Cycle by IDE

the hex file format.

The microcontroller understands machine language consisting of zeroes and ones. Its difficult rather practically impossible for humans to write codes in zeros and ones. Hence we use some high level languages like C, C++, Java, etc. And later a compiler is used to convert these codes into machine language which are stored in a hex file format. A hex file is a text file with the extension .hex.

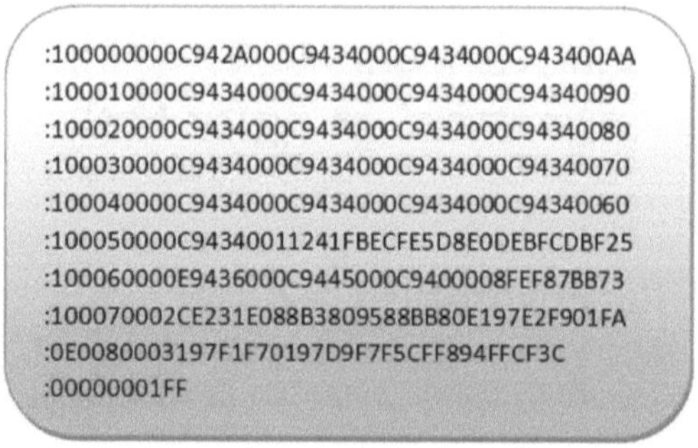

```
:100000000C942A000C9434000C9434000C943400AA
:100010000C9434000C9434000C9434000C94340090
:100020000C9434000C9434000C9434000C94340080
:100030000C9434000C9434000C9434000C94340070
:100040000C9434000C9434000C9434000C94340060
:100050000C94340011241FBECFE5D8E0DEBFCDBF25
:100060000E9436000C9445000C9400008FEF87BB73
:100070002CE231E088B3809588BB80E197E2F901FA
:0E0080003197F1F70197D9F7F5CFF894FFCF3C
:00000001FF
```

Figure 4.5: Hex File Format

The above image shows a typical hex file when opened with notepad or any other text editor. Every line follows a specific structure explained below. : CCAAAAT-TXXXXX......XXSS

Example:

: 100000000C942A000C9434000C9434000C943400AA

1. Every line in a hex file always starts from colon (:)

2. The first two digits CC (Character Count) represent the total number of data byte in that line. Here in this example, 10 (hexadecimal) are the first two digits which mean that there is 16 byte (in decimal) of data in the line.

3. The next four digits represent the starting address of the memory where the data stored in the line needs to be dumped.

4. After address the next two digits represent whether this is the last line of code or not. TT=0, means the code is not complete and there are more lines after this line and TT=1 means this is the last line of the code.

5. XXXX..XX are the data bytes which have to be dumped into the memory. The number of data bytes in a particular line is equal to the number indicated by character count digits (CC).

6. SS is the checksum byte of that line.

The hex file is a text file so one can easily change contents of a hex file. The corrupted line can be identified using the check sum) (SS) byte.

4.10 Programmer/Burner

A programmer/burner is a hardware device accompanied with software which is used to transfer the machine language code to the microcontroller/EEPROM from the PC. The compiler converts the code written in languages like assembly, C, java etc to machine language code (which is understandable by the machines/microcontrollers)

and stores it in a hex file. A programmer acts as an interface between the PC and
the target controller. The API/software of the programmer reads data from the hex
file stored on the PC and feeds it into the controllers memory. The target controller
on which the program needs to be burned is placed on the programmer using a ZIP
socket. The software transfers the data from the PC to the hardware using serial,
parallel or USB port.

Figure 4.6: Interfacing Between PC and Microcontroller

Depending on the way it interacts with PC, the programmers can be classified
into three types:

1. Parallel Programmer: - uses the parallel port of the PC. They are low cost
   programmer but not widely used.

2. Serial Programmers: - uses the serial port to interact with PC via RS232
   protocols. They are more popular among hobbyist working on PC. However
   both the serial and parallel programmers will become obsolete in near future.
   The major reason being unavailability of parallel and serial ports in the PCs
   and Laptops in the coming years.

3. USB Programmer: - uses the USB interface to transfer the data from PC.
   The main advantage of the USB burner is that they are powered from the PC
   itself and there is no need of any additional supply. The USB programmers
   have already become popular and will soon replace the serial and parallel
   programmer.

The programmer generally contains a microcontroller which is preprogrammed to take data from the PC and program the target controller. The programmer burns the target controller using any of the protocols like SPI, parallel interfacing, I2C/TWI or CAN. The speed of burning depends on the way of programmer is interfaced with PC and the protocols used to burn the target controller.

The conventional method to burn a controller is to take it out the circuit, place it on burner and then dump the hex file into the controller using the API. In order to remove this problem of removing the controller from the circuit every time it needs to be programmed, the controllers have now been upgraded with In System Programmer (ISP) feature. This allows burning/programming a controller without removing the controller from the circuit it is used in. The latest controllers are coming with the feature like boot loader memory which allows self burning capabilities, i.e. such controllers do not need any additional programmer hardware. They need only an API to transfer the program to the target controller. This API can also be incorporated in the compiler and hence the compiler can directly burn the target controllers.

Chapter 5

Interface Between RFID With 8051 Microcontroller(AT89c51)

An RFID module basically consists of two parts, namely, a tag and a reader. A typical RFID system consists of an antenna, a transceiver and a transponder (RF tag). The radio frequency is read by the transceiver and the information is transferred to a device for further processing. The information (the unique serial number) to be transmitted is stored in the RF tag or transponder.

The transponder contains a chip and an antenna mounted on a substrate. The chip transmits the relevant information through antenna. The antenna also receives the electromagnetic waves sent by the RFID reader.

Different RFID tags work on different frequencies. Here low frequency, 125 kHz, RFID tags have been used. These tags work within a range of 10 cm. When an RFID tag comes in this range, the reader detects it and sends a unique code of the tag serially. This serial code, consisting of 12 bytes, is received by the microcontroller.

A serial level converter is required for AT89C51 to receive these serial signals. IC MAX232 has been used for this purpose to interface the RFID reader with microcontroller. The circuit connections are as follows:

Receiver1 (R1) of MAX232 has been used for the serial communication. The receiver pin of RFID reader is connected to R1IN (pin13) of MAX232. R1OUT (pin 12) of

MAX232 is connected to RxD (P3.0) of microcontroller.

Table 5.1: Interfacing of RFID With Microcontroller

RFID Reader	MAX232	AT89c51
Rx — R1in	R1in — R1out	R1out — Rx

Pins 1-3 of port P1 (P1.0, P1.1 & P1.2 respectively) of AT89C51 are connected to the control pins 4-6 LCD. The unique identification code of RFID tag is displayed on the LCD.

In the program, Timer1 is configured for serial communication. The baud rate is set to 9600bps for data transmission. The LCD is initialized to display the code. When a card/tag comes in the proximity of RFID reader, the microcontroller reads the code and sends it to the LCD module.

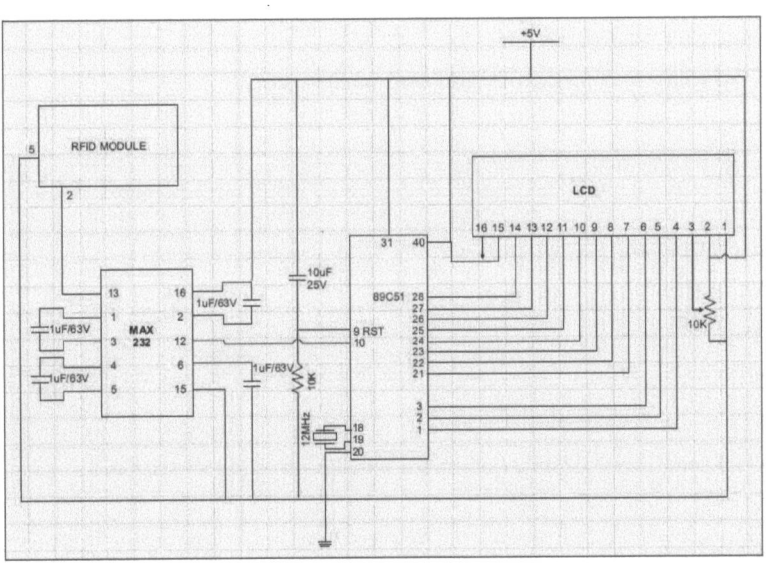

Figure 5.1: Interface Between RFID With 8051 Microcontroller

5.1 Interfacing Code

Program to interface RFID with 8051 microcontroller (AT89C51)

```
#include<stdio.h>
    #include<reg51.h>
    #include<string.h>
    #include"lcd.h"
    unsigned char X[12]=0;//"6E0001B3DC00";
    unsigned char card1[]="6E00018DCF2D";//first card number
    unsigned char card2[]="6E000178E8FF";//second card number
    unsigned char card3[]="6E00012C0447";//third card number
    unsigned char card4[]="6E000A6A313F";//fourth card number
    unsigned char card5[]="6E000A2E470D";//fifth card number
    serial_collect();
    serial_send(char *);
    serial_char_send(char);
    serial_collect()//function to read card number serially {
    unsigned char i;
    for(i=0;i<12;i++)
    {
    while(RI==0);
    X[i]=SBUF;
    RI=0;
    }
    }
    serial_send(char *j)//function to sen infomation on hyper terminal
    {
    while(*j)
    {
    SBUF=*j;
```

```
    while(TI==0);
    TI=0;
    ++j;
}
} void main()
{
TMOD=0X20;//
SCON=0X50;//setting for baud rate selecton of serial communication
TH1=-3;//
TR1=1;//
lcd_init();//function to initialize LCD str_lcd("**welcome to store**");//function to display string on LCD
    delay_msec(100);
    cmd_lcd(0xC0);//command to display on second line of LCD
    delay_msec(100);
    while(1)
    {
    serial_collect();//function to read card number serially if(strncmp(card1,X,12)==0)//function to compare first card number with serially read card number by serial collect() function
        {
        cmd_lcd(0xC0);//command to display on second line of LCD
        delay_msec(100);
        str_lcd(" Rana Dipesh H");//function to display string on LCD
        //delay_msec(100);
        cmd_lcd(0x94);//command to display on second line of LCD
        delay_msec(100);
        str_lcd("BE(E&TC) ROLL NO-95 ");
        delay_msec(100); serial_send("6E00018DCF2D");
        delay_msec(100);
```

```
cmd_lcd(0x0D4);
str_lcd("**Thanks for visit**");
}
else if(strncmp(card2,X,12)==0)//function to compare second card number with serially read card number by serial_collect() function
{
cmd_lcd(0xC0);//command to display on second line of LCD
delay_msec(100);
str_lcd(" Shukla Anand K ");//function to display string on LCD
delay_msec(100);
cmd_lcd(0x94);//command to display on second line of LCD
delay_msec(100); str_lcd("BE(E&TC)ROLL NO-106 ");
delay_msec(100);
serial_send("6E000178E8FF");
cmd_lcd(0x0D4);
delay_msec(100);
str_lcd("**Thanks for visit**");
}
else if(strncmp(card3,X,12)==0)//function to compare third card number with serially read card number by serial_collect() function
{
cmd_lcd(0xC0);//command to display on second line of LCD
delay_msec(100);
str_lcd(" Musale Rakesh S ");//function to display string on LCD
delay_msec(100);
cmd_lcd(0x94);//command to display on second line of LCD
delay_msec(100);
str_lcd("BE(E&TC)ROLL NO-127 ");
delay_msec(100);
serial_send("6E00012C0447");
```

```c
cmd_lcd(0x0D4);
delay_msec(100);
str_lcd("**Thanks for visit**");
} else if(strncmp(card4,X,12)==0)//function to compare fourth card number with serially read card number by serial_collect() function
{
cmd_lcd(0xC0);//command to display on second line of LCD
delay_msec(100);
str_lcd(" P. R. Bhole ");//function to display string on LCD
delay_msec(100);
cmd_lcd(0x94);//command to display on second line of LCD
delay_msec(100);
str_lcd(" Project Guide ");
delay_msec(100);
serial_send("6E000A6A313F");
cmd_lcd(0x0D4);
delay_msec(100);
str_lcd("**Thanks for visit**");
}
else if(strncmp(card5,X,12)==0)//function to compare fifth card number with serially read card number by serial_collect() function
{
cmd_lcd(0xC0);//command to display on second line of LCD
delay_msec(100);
str_lcd(" name of student1 ");//function to display string on LCD
delay_msec(100); cmd_lcd(0x94);//command to display on second line of LCD
delay_msec(100);
str_lcd("BE(E&TC)ROLL NO- ");
delay_msec(100);
serial_send("6E000A2E470D");
```

```
cmd_lcd(0X0D4);
delay_msec(100);
str_lcd("**Thanks for visit**");
} // else if end
else
{
cmd_lcd(0xC0);//command to display on second line of LCD
delay_msec(100);
str_lcd("No card match found "); cmd_lcd(0x94);//command to display on second line of LCD
delay_msec(100);
str_lcd("Please check card ");//function to display string on LCD
}//else end
} //while end*/
}//main end
```

Chapter 6

Database Management System and .Net Framework

A general-purpose **database management system (DBMS)** is a software system designed to allow the definition, creation, querying, update, and administration of databases. Well-known DBMSs include MySQL, PostgreSQL, SQLite, Microsoft SQL Server, Microsoft Access, Oracle, Sybase, dBASE, FoxPro, and IBM DB2. A database is not generally portable across different DBMS, but different DBMSs can inter-operate by using standards such as SQL and ODBC or JDBC to allow a single application to work with more than one database.

The **.NET Framework's** Base Class Library provides user interface, data access, database connectivity, cryptography, web application development, numeric algorithms, and network communications. Programmers produce software by combining their own source code with the .NET Framework and other libraries. The .NET Framework is intended to be used by most new applications created for the Windows platform. Microsoft also produces an integrated development environment largely for .NET software called Visual Studio.

6.1 Database

A database is an organized collection of data. The data is typically organized to model relevant aspects of reality (for example, the availability of rooms in hotels), in a way that supports processes requiring this information (for example, finding a hotel with vacancies).

6.2 Terminology and Overview

Formally, the term "database" refers to the data itself and supporting data structures. A "database management system" (DBMS) is a suite of computer software providing the interface between users and a database or databases. Because they are so closely related, the term "database" when used casually often refers to both a DBMS and the data it manipulates.

Outside the world of professional information technology, the term database is sometimes used casually to refer to any collection of data (perhaps a spreadsheet, maybe even a card index). This article is concerned only with databases where the size and usage requirements necessitate use of a database management system.[1] The interactions catered for by most existing DBMS fall into four main groups:

- Data definition. Defining new data structures for a database, removing data structures from the database, modifying the structure of existing data.

- Update. Inserting, modifying, and deleting data.

- Retrieval. Obtaining information either for end-user queries and reports or for processing by applications.

- Administration. Registering and monitoring users, enforcing data security, monitoring performance, maintaining data integrity, dealing with concurrency control, and recovering information if the system fails.

A DBMS is responsible for maintaining the integrity and security of stored data, and for recovering information if the system fails. Both a database and its DBMS conform to the principles of a particular database model. "Database system" refers collectively to the database model, database management system, and database. Physically, database servers are dedicated computers that hold the actual databases and run only the DBMS and related software. Database servers are usually multi-processor computers, with generous memory and RAID disk arrays used for stable storage. Hardware database accelerators, connected to one or more servers via a high-speed channel, are also used in large volume transaction processing environments. DBMSs are found at the heart of most database applications. DBMSs may be built around a custom multitasking kernel with built-in networking support, but modern DBMSs typically rely on a standard operating system to provide these functions. [citation needed] Since DBMSs comprise a significant economical market, computer and storage vendors often take into account DBMS requirements in their own development plans.[citation needed].

Databases and DBMSs can be categorized according to the database model(s) that they support (such as relational or XML), the type(s) of computer they run on (from a server cluster to a mobile phone), the query language(s) used to access the database (such as SQL or XQuery), and their internal engineering, which affects performance, scaleability, resilience, and security.

6.3 Applications and Roles

Most organizations in developed countries today depend on databases for their business operations. Increasingly, databases are not only used to support the internal operations of the organization, but also to underpin its online interactions with customers and suppliers (see Enterprise software). Databases are not used only to hold administrative information, but are often embedded within applications to hold more specialized data: for example engineering data or economic models. Examples of database applications include computerized library systems, flight reservation systems, and computerized parts inventory systems. Client-server or transactional DBMSs are often complex to maintain high performance, availability and security when many users are querying and updating the database at the same time. Personal, desktop-based database systems tend to be less complex. For example, FileMaker and Microsoft Access come with built-in graphical user interfaces.

6.4 Database Design and Modelling

The first task of a database designer is to produce a conceptual data model that reflects the structure of the information to be held in the database. A common approach to this is to develop an entity-relationship model, often with the aid of drawing tools. Another popular approach is the Unified Modeling Language. A successful data model will accurately reflect the possible state of the external world being modeled: for example, if people can have more than one phone number, it will allow this information to be captured. Designing a good conceptual data model requires a good understanding of the application domain; it typically involves asking deep questions about the things of interest to an organisation, like "can a customer also be a supplier?", or "if a product is sold with two different forms of packaging, are those the same product or different products?", or "if a plane flies from New York to Dubai via Frankfurt, is that one flight or two (or maybe even three)?". The answers to these questions establish definitions of the terminology used for entities (customers, products, flights, flight segments) and their relationships and attributes.

The most popular database model for general-purpose databases is the relational model, or more precisely, the relational model as represented by the SQL language. The process of creating a logical database design using this model uses a methodical approach known as normalization. The goal of normalization is to ensure that each elementary "fact" is only recorded in one place, so that insertions, updates, and deletions automatically maintain consistency.

The final stage of database design is to make the decisions that affect performance, scaleability, recovery, security, and the like. This is often called physical database design. A key goal during this stage is data independence, meaning that the decisions made for performance optimization purposes should be invisible to end-users and applications. Physical design is driven mainly by performance requirements, and requires a good knowledge of the expected workload and access patterns, and a deep understanding of the features offered by the chosen DBMS.

Another aspect of physical database design is security. It involves both defining access control to database objects as well as defining security levels and methods for the data itself.

6.5 Database Models

Collage of five types of database models. A database model is a type of data model that determines the logical structure of a database and fundamentally determines in which manner data can be stored, organized, and manipulated. The most popular example of a database model is the relational model (or the SQL approximation of relational), which uses a table-based format.

Common logical data models for databases include:

- Hierarchical database model

- Network model

- Relational model

- Entityrelationship model

- Enhanced entityrelationship model

- Object model

- Document model

- Entityattributevalue model

- Star schema

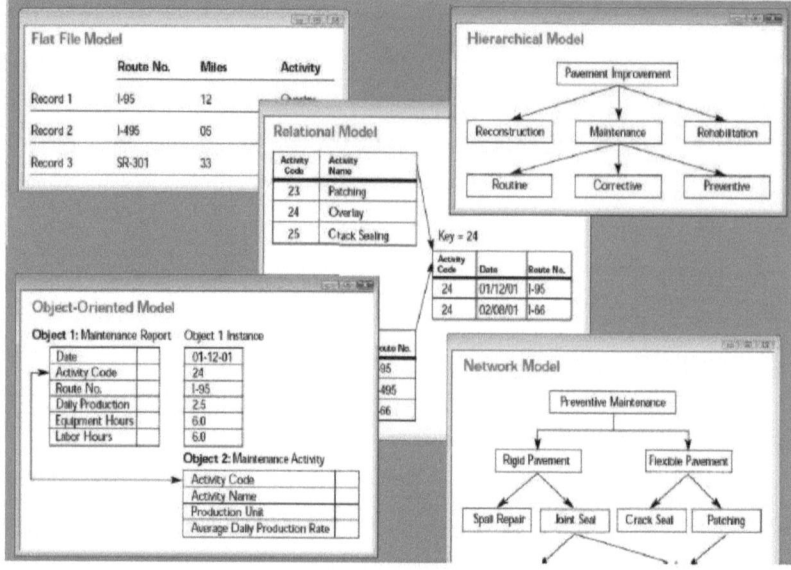

Figure 6.1: Collage of Five types of Database

An object-relational database combines the two related structures.
Physical data models include:

- Inverted index

- Flat file

Other models include:

- Associative model

- Multidimensional model

- Multivalue model

- Semantic model

- XML database

- Named graph

6.6 Database Storage

Database storage is the container of the physical materialization of a database. It comprises the internal (physical) level in the database architecture. It also contains all the information needed (e.g., metadata, "data about the data", and internal data structures) to reconstruct the conceptual level and external level from the internal level when needed. Putting data into permanent storage is generally the responsibility of the database engine a.k.a. "storage engine". Though typically accessed by a DBMS through the underlying operating system (and often utilizing the operating systems' file systems as intermediates for storage layout), storage properties and configuration setting are extremely important for the efficient operation of the DBMS, and thus are closely maintained by database administrators. A DBMS, while in operation, always has its database residing in several types of storage (e.g., memory and external storage). The database data and the additional needed information, possibly in very large amounts, are coded into bits. Data typically reside in the storage in structures that look completely different from the way the data look in the conceptual and external levels, but in ways that attempt to optimize (the best possible) these levels' reconstruction when needed by users and programs, as well as for computing additional types of needed information from the data (e.g., when querying the database). Some DBMS support specifying which character encoding was used to store data, so multiple encodings can be used in the same database.

Various low-level database storage structures are used by the storage engine to serialize the data model so it can be written to the medium of choice. Techniques such as indexing may be used to improve performance. Conventional storage is row-oriented, but there are also column-oriented and correlation databases.

6.7 Database Security

Database security deals with all various aspects of protecting the database content, its owners, and its users. It ranges from protection from intentional unauthorized database uses to unintentional database accesses by unauthorized entities (e.g., a person or a computer program).

Database access control deals with controlling who (a person or a certain computer program) is allowed to access what information in the database. The information may comprise specific database objects (e.g., record types, specific records, data structures), certain computations over certain objects (e.g., query types, or specific queries), or utilizing specific access paths to the former (e.g., using specific indexes or other data structures to access information). Database access controls are set by special authorized (by the database owner) personnel that uses dedicated protected security DBMS interfaces.

This may be managed directly on an individual basis, or by the assignment of individuals and privileges to groups, or (in the most elaborate models) through the assignment of individuals and groups to roles which are then granted entitlements. Data security prevents unauthorized users from viewing or updating the database. Using passwords, users are allowed access to the entire database or subsets of it called "subschemas". For example, an employee database can contain all the data about an individual employee, but one group of users may be authorized to view only payroll data, while others are allowed access to only work history and medical data. If the DBMS provides a way to interactively enter and update the database, as well as interrogate it, this capability allows for managing personal databases.

Data security in general deals with protecting specific chunks of data, both physically (i.e., from corruption, or destruction, or removal; e.g., see physical security), or the interpretation of them, or parts of them to meaningful information (e.g., by looking at the strings of bits that they comprise, concluding specific valid credit-card numbers; e.g., see data encryption).

Change and access logging records who accessed which attributes, what was changed, and when it was changed. Logging services allow for a forensic database audit later by keeping a record of access occurrences and changes. Sometimes application-level code is used to record changes rather than leaving this to the database. Monitoring can be set up to attempt to detect security breaches.

6.8 .Net Framework

The .NET Framework (pronounced dot net) is a software framework developed by Microsoft that runs primarily on Microsoft Windows. It includes a large library and provides language interoperability (each language can use code written in other languages) across several programming languages. Programs written for the .NET Framework execute in a software environment (as contrasted to hardware environment), known as the Common Language Runtime (CLR), an application virtual machine that provides services such as security, memory management, and exception handling. The class library and the CLR together constitute the .NET Framework. Microsoft started development of the .NET Framework in the late 1990s, originally under the name of Next Generation Windows Services (NGWS). By late 2000 the first beta versions of .NET 1.0 were released. Version 3.0 of the .NET Framework is included with Windows Server 2008 and Windows Vista. Version 3.5 is included with Windows 7 and Windows Server 2008 R2, and can also be installed on Windows XP and Windows Server 2003.[2] On 12 April 2010, .NET Framework 4 was released alongside Visual Studio 2.

The .NET Framework family also includes two versions for mobile or embedded device use. A reduced version of the framework, the .NET Compact Framework, is available on Windows CE platforms, including Windows Mobile devices such as smartphones. Additionally, the .NET Micro Framework is targeted at severely resource-constrained devices.

6.9 Design Features

- Interoperability:- Because computer systems commonly require interaction between newer and older applications, the .NET Framework provides means to access functionality implemented in newer and older programs that execute outside the .NET environment. Access to COM components is provided in the System. Runtime. Interop Services and System.EnterpriseServices names-

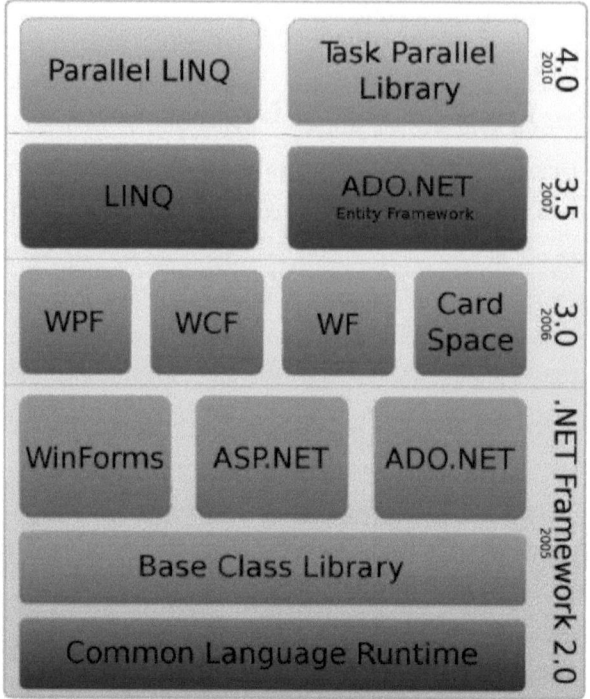

Figure 6.2: The .NET Framework Stack

paces of the framework; access to other functionality is achieved using the P/Invoke feature.

- Common Language Runtime engine:- The Common Language Runtime (CLR) serves as the execution engine of the .NET Framework. All .NET programs execute under the supervision of the CLR, guaranteeing certain properties and behaviors in the areas of memory management, security, and exception handling.

- Language independence:- The .NET Framework introduces a Common Type System, or CTS. The CTS specification defines all possible datatypes and programming constructs supported by the CLR and how they may or may not interact with each other conforming to the Common Language Infrastructure (CLI) specification. Because of this feature, the .NET Framework supports the exchange of types and object instances between libraries and applications written using any conforming .NET language.

- Base Class Library:- The Base Class Library (BCL), part of the Framework Class Library (FCL), is a library of functionality available to all languages using the .NET Framework. The BCL provides classes that encapsulate a number of common functions, including file reading and writing, graphic rendering, database interaction, XML document manipulation, and so on. It consists of classes, interfaces of reusable types that integrates with CLR(Common Language Runtime).

- Simplified deployment:- The .NET Framework includes design features and tools which help manage the installation of computer software to ensure it does not interfere with previously installed software, and it conforms to security requirements.

- Security:- The design addresses some of the vulnerabilities, such as buffer overflows, which have been exploited by malicious software. Additionally, .NET provides a common security model for all applications.

- Portability:- While Microsoft has never implemented the full framework on any system except Microsoft Windows, it has engineered the framework to be platform-agnostic,and cross-platform implementations are available for other operating systems (see Silverlight and the Alternative implementations section below). Microsoft submitted the specifications for the Common Language Infrastructure (which includes the core class libraries, Common Type System, and the Common Intermediate Language), the C# language,and the C++/CLI language to both ECMA and the ISO, making them available as official standards. This makes it possible for third parties to create compatible implementations of the framework and its languages on other platforms.

6.10 Common Language Infrastructure(CLI)

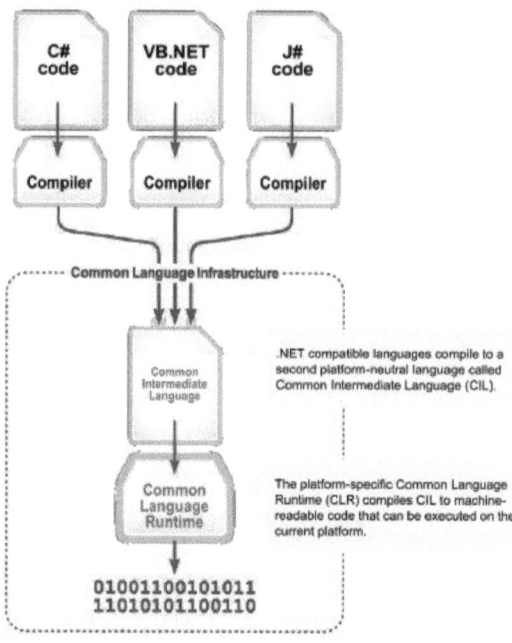

Figure 6.3: Visual overview of the Common Language Infrastructure(CLI)

The purpose of the Common Language Infrastructure (CLI) is to provide a language-neutral platform for application development and execution, including functions for Exception handling, Garbage Collection, security, and interoperability. By implementing the core aspects of the .NET Framework within the scope of the CL, this functionality will not be tied to a single language but will be available across the many languages supported by the framework. Microsoft's implementation of the CLI is called the Common Language Runtime, or CLR.

The CIL code is housed in CLI assemblies. As mandated by the specification, assemblies are stored in the Portable Executable (PE) format, common on the Windows platform for all DLL and EXE files. The assembly consists of one or more files, one of which must contain the manifest, which has the metadata for the assembly. The complete name of an assembly (not to be confused with the filename on disk) contains its simple text name, version number, culture, and public key token. Assemblies are considered equivalent if they share the same complete name, excluding the revision of the version number. A private key can also be used by the creator of the assembly for strong naming. The public key token identifies which public key an assembly is signed with. Only the creator of the keypair (typically the .NET developer signing the assembly) can sign assemblies that have the same strong name as a previous version assembly, since he is in possession of the private key. Strong naming is required to add assemblies to the Global Assembly Cache.

6.11 Security

.NET has its own security mechanism with 2 general features: Code Access Security (CAS), and validation and verification. Code Access Security is based on evidence that is associated with a specific assembly. Typically the evidence is the source of the assembly (whether it is installed on the local machine or has been downloaded from the intranet or Internet). Code Access Security uses evidence to determine the permissions granted to the code. Other code can demand that calling code is granted a specified permission. The demand causes the CLR to perform a call stack walk: every assembly of each method in the call stack is checked for the required permission; if any assembly is not granted the permission a security exception is thrown.

6.12 Availability

While the standards that make up .NET are inherently cross-platform, Microsoft's full implementation of .NET is supported only on Microsoft Windows.

Chapter 7

Main Circuit and Design

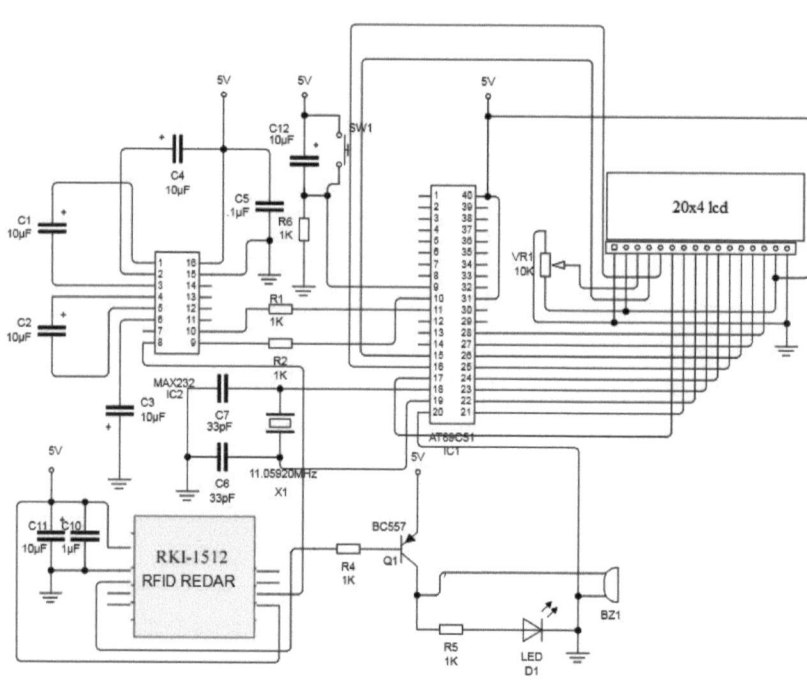

Figure 7.1: Circuit of Digital Receipt System

Table 7.1: Component List

Sr. No.	Components	Specifications
1.	Atmel-89c51	
2.	RFID reader	
3.	RFID Tag	
4.	LCD Module	20×4
5.	Max-232	
6.	RS-232 Serial Cable	
7.	DB-9 Connector	
8.	Breadboard	
9.	Transformer	12-0-12V, 230V, 50Hz
10.	Regulator IC-7805	
11.	Two pin Connector	
12.	Diode	$1N4007 \times 4$
13.	PNP Transistor	BC-557
14.	Capacitor	$1000\mu f(16v) \times 1$ $10\mu f(16v) \times 2$ $10\mu f(50v) \times 4$ $4.7\mu f \times 4$ $100\mu f \times 1$ $0.1\mu f \times 1$ $33\mu f \times 2$
15.	Resistor	$560\Omega \times 2$ $1K\Omega \times 1$ $150\Omega \times 1$ $470\Omega \times 1$
16.	IC Base	$40\text{pin} \times 1$ $16\text{pin} \times 1$
17.	Female Strip (For LCD & RFID)	
18.	Male Strip (For LCD)	
19.	X'tal(11.0592 MHz)	
20.	Push Buttons	3
21.	Red LED	
22.	Buzzer	
23.	Connecting wires	
24.	Trim Pot	

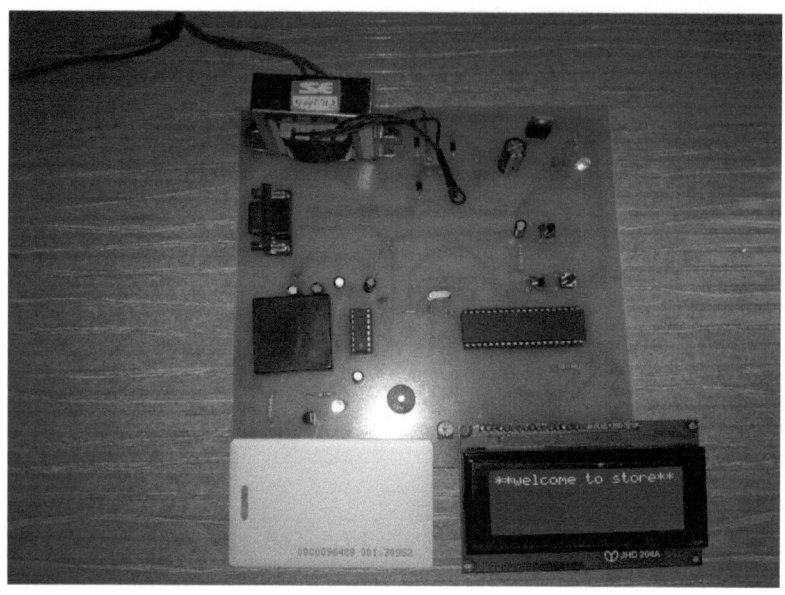

Figure 7.2: Model of Digital Receipt System

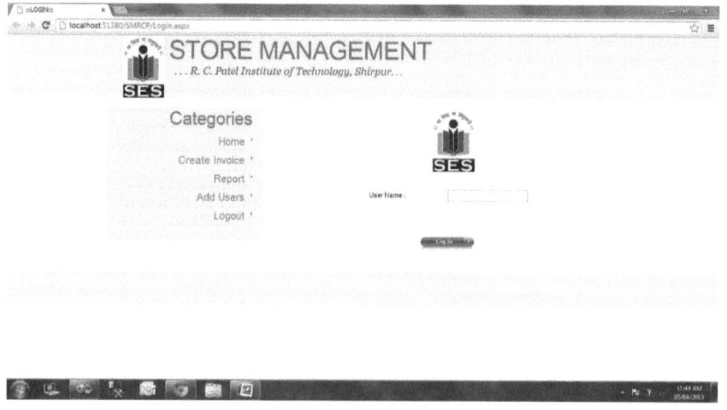

Figure 7.3: LOGIN

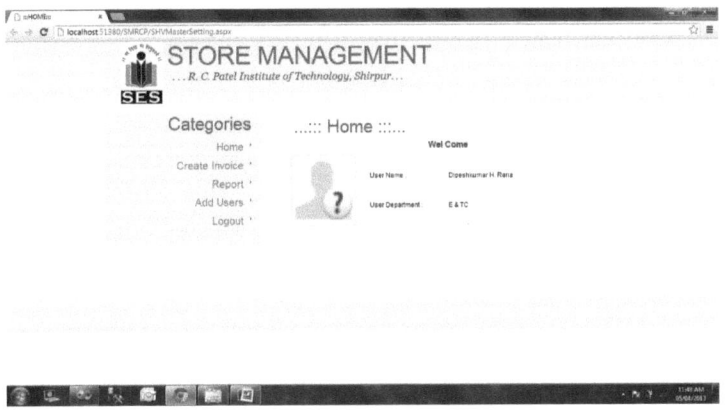

Figure 7.4: HOME

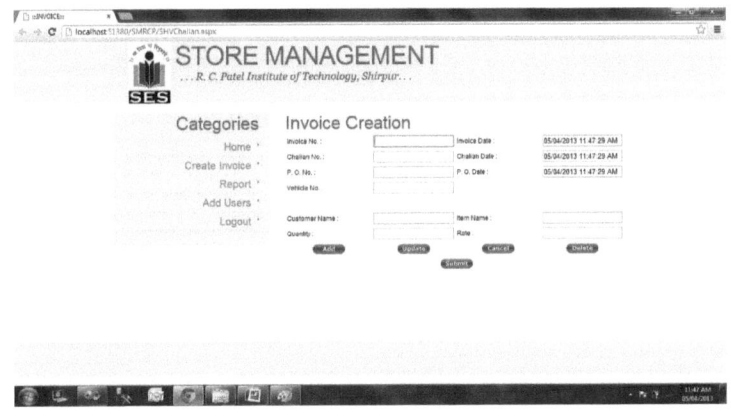

Figure 7.5: INVOICE

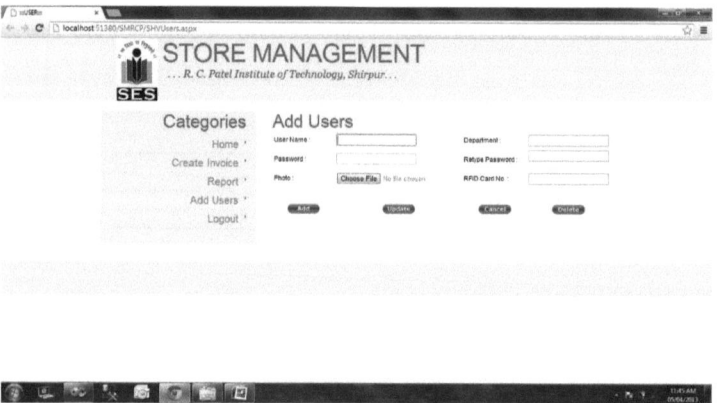

Figure 7.6: ADD USER

Chapter 8

Testing Results

Table 8.1: Power Supply Section

Component	Vtg/ImA
Across Transformers Secondary o/p	6.6V,300mA
Across Rectifier	6.42V
Across 7805	4.92V

Table 8.2: RFID Section

Card No.	Name(Databse)
6E00018DCF2D	Rana Dipesh H BE(E & TC) Roll No-95
6E00017E8FF	Shukla Anand K BE(E & TC) Roll No-106
6E00012C0447	Musale Rakesh S BE(E & TC) Roll No-127

Table 8.3: LCD Section

Item	Vtg/ImA
Input Voltage	2.2 V
output Voltage/current	2.2,0.2mA

Our project successfully read the RFID tag, compare its number with the number stored in the micro controller and display the name,branch and roll no. on the LCD display. It also send that number to the computer through RS-232 serial cable and open the database of that student.

1. Speed of Execution

   our digital receipt system prototype competed read an RFID tagin about a second, and database access over RS-232 took less than 1 second. In all,the user would be strictly" Waiting" only for a total of about 2 seconds. Ofcours, this 2 seconds Does not takes into a account the time that the cashier takes to enter the amount or the time that the user takes to enter his/her security pin. In order to make the RFID reading quicker we would need to reduce the number of times we check the tag.We did not want to reduce the number of checks from 20 to say 5, but that would also reduce the accuracy of the system.

2. Accuracy

   We had n accuracy of 80% .We had no false positives ,as we would check the same tag no. of times in order to make sure that the ID is actually the same. However, depending on the angle in which the tag is held in front of the RFID reader coil,we did have a false negatives. now, we could account for this in Software but we can't find any hardware method to detect the scenario. In the eventual commercial application, when the tag is used a sticker on the user's ID,users could simply be prompted to bring their ID within a 1" reading distance.

3. Safety

   This device does not pose any safety or health threats to its users. We have an insulating box as the container for the system and the user interacts with the device only through the keypad, which is made out of insulating plastics. There are power and RS-232 Cables that are connected to the device and this component cant inflict harm upon the user as the user does not interact with this cables.

Chapter 9

Conclusion and Future Scope

As Per the requirement we expect that our project is made for the access of database of every student in collage component store.

We make our project like this way that every student who issue their ID card made up of RFID tag can use that card for the purchasing of any component from the store.Entry of purchased component will be stored in the database of the store.

When student place the card in front of the RFID reader, the reader compare the card number with the number stored in the database.If the number is matched then the database of student will open and name, branch and roll number of the student will flash on the LCD, and the purchased entry of that student will be store in it and student can get receipt of their purchased component.

Without its ID card no one can access his/her database.

In terms of usability, the system was easy and smooth to operate so long as card swipes were done smoothly. On the MCU side, the status messages on the LCD served as visual cues for what the program was currently doing. On the database interface side, logging in, viewing transactions, and logging out are also simple, partially because those are the only operations.

For the Futuristic use of this system it can be implemented in the Libraries, Schools, Departmental stores,Medical Stores.It can be also implementable online that customers can have their purchased details and bill on their Laptops and Smart phones.

References

[1] J. Pereira, M. Teixeira, Porqu E-commerce

[2] Kyong Jun Lee, Jeong-In Ju, Jeong Mu Jeong, A Payment & Receipt Business Model in U-Commerce Environment, ACM International Conference Proceeding Series; Vol156,ACM,2006.

[3] Carl S. Marshall, Adam T. Lake, Rosa J. Thanasohon, Mobile Digital Receipts, US 2003/0055733 A1, 2003

[4] Jeffrey Ullman 1997: First course in database systems, Prentice-Hall Inc., Simon & Schuster, Page 1, ISBN 0-13-861337-0.

[5] Tsitchizris, D. C. and F. H. Lochovsky (1982). Data Models. Englewood-Cliffs, Prentice-Hall.

[6] Beynon-Davies P. (2004). Database Systems 3rd Edition. Palgrave, Basingstoke, UK. ISBN 1-4039-1601-2